Withdrawn

Text written by Martin Manser and Alice Grandison

Illustrated by Jan Smith

Designed by Fiona Grant

Edited in the U.K. by Vicci Parr

Edited in the U.S. by Joanna Callihan

Mc Graw Hill **Children's Publishing**

This edition published in the United States of America
in 2003 by Waterbird Books,
an imprint of McGraw-Hill Children's Publishing,
a Division of The McGraw-Hill Companies
8787 Orion Place
Columbus, Ohio 43240-4027

www.MHkids.com

Library of Congress Cataloging-in-Publication Data is on file with the publisher

Printed in China.

1-57768-557-1

1 2 3 4 5 6 7 8 9 10 BRI 09 08 07 06 05 04 03

Getting to Grips with Grammar

WATERBIRD BOOKS

Columbus, Ohio

Nouns

A **noun** is a "naming" word. It tells you what a person, place, or thing is. For example, *ball, cat*, and *girl* are all nouns.

A **singular noun** is a word for one thing. For example, in this sentence, *cake* is a singular noun: *Tom ate a cake.*

A **plural noun** is a word for more than one thing. In this sentence, *cakes* is a plural noun: *Lucy ate six cakes.*

In most cases, you make a noun plural by adding the letter *s* to the end of the word.

An **irregular plural noun** can refer to more than one thing, without adding an *s*. An example of this is the sentence: *I saw two deer.*

streamers

balloons

hat

Robert

Stacy

badge

sandwiches

cakes

pizza

plate

table

fish

mom

cake

chair

ice cream

presents

A **proper noun** is a kind of noun that is a name. For example, it can be the name of a person, a place, or a day or month. A proper noun always begins with a capital letter.

Nouns that are not proper nouns are called **common nouns.**

In this phrase, *The city of Paris, city* is a common noun, and *Paris* is a proper noun.

Verbs

A **verb** is an "action" word. It tells you what a person or thing does. For example, *jump, run,* and *swim* are all verbs.

Grandma writes postcards.

Ryan and Sophie eat ice cream.

A man *sells* drinks and ice cream.

Carly sunbathes.

Rachel collects seashells.

Harry waves to his mom.

Chloe and her dad *wade* in the water.

The sun *shines* in the sky.

Sam *flies* a kite.

A boat *sails* past.

Louise *throws* a disk.

A seagull *catches* a fish.

Jack and Emma *bury* their dad in the sand.

Susie *builds* a sandcastle.

The dog *splashes* the children.

The crab *runs* along the beach.

Children *swim* in the ocean.

9

Verb Tenses

The tense of a verb tells you when an action occurs. A verb can be in the **past tense**, the **present tense**, or the **future tense**.

John *painted* the fence.

Tom *herded* the sheep.

past

The past tense tells you about something that has already happened. In most cases, you make the past tense by adding *ed* to the end of the verb.

The farmer *plows* the field.

present

The cat *will chase* the ducks.

Katie will *brush* the dog.

Lauren *milks* the cow.

future

The present tense tells you about something that is happening now.

The future tense tells you about something that will happen. You make the future tense by putting *will* before the verb.

11

Adjectives

An **adjective** is a "describing" word. It tells you more about a noun. It tells you what a thing or a person looks like, feels like, or sounds like.

green trees

a *good* game

a *red* slide

a *happy* boy

a *tall* girl

a *short* girl

a *fast* skateboarder

12

two swings

dark hair

blond hair

a *sad* girl

a *big* smile

a *blue* hat

a black and white ball

six seats

a *spinning* merry-go-round

Color adjectives tell you what color something is. For example, when you say *a red apple, red* is an adjective.

Number adjectives tell you how many of something there are. For example, when you say *six pencils, six* is an adjective.

13

Opposites

Opposite words describe things that are completely different from each other. Opposite words are also called **antonyms.**

Paul is happy.

Jenny is sad.

Look at the pictures below. Each picture in the top row has an antonym in the bottom row.

fat

little

asleep

hot

long

thin

big

awake

cold

short

Comparisons

Comparison words are used to describe two or more people, places or things.

Bill is tall. Harry is taller than Bill. Alex is the tallest of the three boys.

Taller is the **comparative** of *tall.* Use the comparative form when you are comparing two items.

Tallest is the **superlative** of *tall.* Use the superlative form when you are comparing three or more items.

15

Adverbs

An **adverb** tells you more about a verb. It tells you how, when, or where something is done. Look at the park and see how many adverbs you can find.

Many adverbs are made by adding *ly* to the end of an adjective.

adjective	+ ly =	adverb
slow	+ ly =	slowly
clever	+ ly =	cleverly
sad	+ ly =	sadly

Although most adverbs end in *ly*, there are a few that do not. For example, *fast*, *hard*, and *high* can be adverbs. In this sentence, *Paul works hard*, *hard* is an adverb. It tells you more about the verb *works*. How does Paul work? He works hard.

16

The old man walks slowly.

The children skate fast.

The boy kicks the ball hard.

The children play happily.

The balloon floats *high*.

The ducks quack *loudly*.

Grandma is leaning *forward*.

The dog digs *quickly*.

Mom *gently* rocks the stroller.

Dad sleeps *peacefully*.

17

Pronouns

A **pronoun** is a short word that takes the place of a noun.
You use a pronoun rather than repeating a noun.

She prefers her cat.

He likes biscuits.

I love my pet mouse.

Becky is afraid of *it*.

Personal pronouns are used for people, animals, or things:

I   you   he   she   it   we   they   me   him   her   us   them

Our family.

Lucy loves _her_ magazines.

His sandwich looks good.

Their television is huge!

These videos are _ours_.

This is _my_ toy.

Possessive pronouns are used to show ownership:
my   mine   your   yours   his   her   hers   its   our   ours   their   theirs

Prepositions

The light hangs *from* the ceiling.

The bookcase is *against* the wall.

The moon is *outside* the window.

The toys are *in* the toy box.

A **preposition** shows you how a thing or a person relates to something else.
For example, *on, under,* and *beside* are all prepositions.

The picture is *above* the bed.

Sarah is *in* bed.

The dog is *on* the bed.

The slippers are *under* the bed.

The cat is *behind* the door.

Sarah read her book *before* she went to sleep.

Prepositions can also tell you when something happens. For example, *before*, *after*, and *in* are all prepositions.

Sentences

A **sentence** is a group of words that make complete sense together. A sentence tells you something, or asks a question. Sentences always begin with a capital letter and usually end in a period.

A sentence must include a verb (an action word) and at least one noun (a naming word) or pronoun (a word that takes the place of a noun).

One type of sentence is called a **statement**. A statement tells you something. It begins with a capital letter and ends with a period.

It is raining.

There is another kind of sentence called a **question**. A question asks something. A question also begins with a capital letter, but it ends with a question mark instead of a period.

Is it raining?

The boy went to bed.

He was tired.

"Are you asleep?" Mom asked.

Is this paint wet?

The bedroom is messy.

Punctuation

Punctuation is important because it makes sentences and words easier to understand and read. Punctuation helps to break up sentences and shows where they end.

A **period** is a mark that looks like a dot. You write a period at the end of a sentence.

A **question mark** is a mark that looks like this: ?. If you write a sentence that is a question, you use a question mark at the end instead of a period.

Questions words are words that are often used at the beginning of a question. These words are:
who   what   which   when   where   why   how

An **exclamation mark** is a mark that looks like this: !. If you write a sentence that is a surprise, or expresses strong feeling such as pain or anger, use an exclamation mark at the end instead of a period.

The birds are singing.

It is very hot.

Hello!

24

25

Speech

When you write something that someone else has said, you need to use special punctuation marks called **quotation marks**. These are also used when you are writing a story and want to write what a character says. Quotation marks always come in pairs. For example, *Molly said, "I am hungry."*

You use a **comma** after the unspoken words and before the spoken words. Commas are helpful, especially when reading aloud because they tell you when to pause. *The teacher shouted, "Be quiet!"*

An **apostrophe** appears inside a word to indicate a missing letter or letters. For example, *don't* really means *do not*. Apostrophes are also used to show ownership of something. *I went to Bob's house.* In this sentence, the apostrophe is used to show that the house belongs to Bob.

Maria screamed, "That's not your bike!"

"I'm going really fast!" the boy said.

What is a dictionary?

A **dictionary** is a book that contains lots of words and their definitions. The words are organized in alphabetical order.

Alphabetical order means that words are arranged in ABC order, starting with their first letter. For example, *apple* comes before *banana*. If two words begin with the same letter, then the order depends on the second letter, and so on. For example, *daisy* comes before *doll*.

Why should I use a dictionary?

You can use a dictionary if you need help with:

* the meaning of a word
* the spelling of a word
* how to pronounce a word
* how to use the word in a sentence, including what part of speech the word is

How do I use a dictionary?

When you first open a dictionary, follow the alphabetical order rule to find the word that you are looking for. Then look closely at all the information given for that word.

word

how to pronounce the word

what part of speech it is

Fence /fens/ noun
1. a barrier of wire or boards to prevent escape.
　2. an obstacle jumped by a horse.

Second meaning of word

First meaning of word

29